With blessings to my friend

_____

I thank God
for the gift of your friendship.

May God bless you and keep you
And make his face shine brightly upon you
Today and always.

Thanks for the gift of you!

Your Friend,

_____

_____

date

Stories, sayings, and Scriptures to Encourage and Inspire

hugs
for
friends

Stories and Personalized Scriptures by
LeAnn Weiss

Messages by
Caron Loveless

HOWARD
PUBLISHING CO.

Our purpose at Howard Books is to:

- *Increase faith* in the hearts of growing Christians
- *Inspire holiness* in the lives of believers
- *Instill hope* in the hearts of struggling people everywhere

Because He's coming again!

HOWARD BOOKS

Published by Howard Books, a division of Simon & Schuster, Inc.
1230 Avenue of the Americas, New York, NY 10020
www.howardpublishing.com

Hugs for Friends © 1999 by LeAnn Weiss

Personalized scriptures by LeAnn Weiss, owner of Encouragement Company
3006 Brandywine Dr., Orlando, FL 32806; 407-898-4410

Library of Congress Cataloging-in-Publication Data

Weiss, LeAnn.
    Hugs for friends : stories, sayings, and scriptures to encourage and inspire,/
LeAnn Weiss.
        p. cm.
    10 Digit ISBN 1-58229-006-7
    10 Digit ISBN 1-4165-3336-2
    1. Friendship—Religious aspects—Christianity. I. Title.
BV4647.F7W385 1999
242—dc21   98-33367
                                             CIP

38 37 36 35 34 33 32 31

Manufactured in the United States of America

For information regarding special discounts for bulk purchases, please contact: Simon & Schuster Special Sales at 1-800-456-6798 or business@simonandschuster.com.

Interior design by LinDee Loveland
Edited by Philis Boultinghouse

Scripture references are from the THE HOLY BIBLE: AMERICAN STANDARD VERSION. Copyright © 1901 (expired) by Thomas Nelson & Sons unless otherwise marked.

Contents

A friend is the hope of the heart.

—Ralph Waldo Emerson

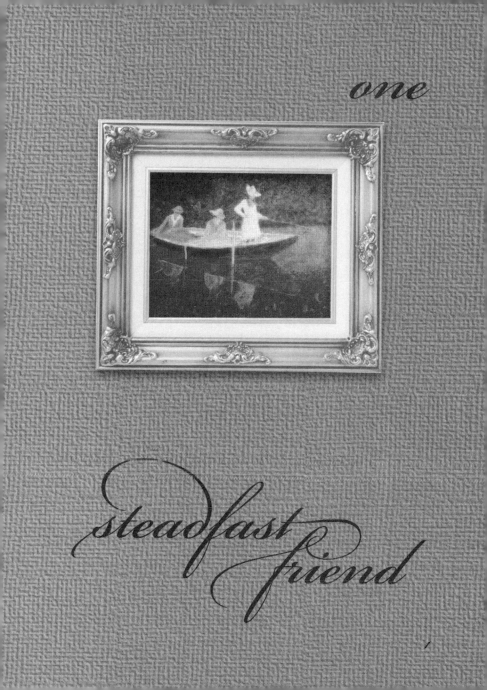

one

steadfast
friend

Catch a glimpse
of my *incredible* love for you!

I pray that you, being rooted and established
in love, may have the power to grasp
how **wide**

and *long*

and **high**

and **deep** is my completely

unconditional love for you—

a *love* that surpasses all human knowledge.

My forever love, *Jesus*

—Ephesians 3:17–19

Friends possess remarkable keys. They open the locked doors of our lives. They give us entrance to places we'd never dare go by ourselves. They fling wide the gates of lush, secret gardens. They take us to treasure rooms glistening with gifts we're sure we don't deserve.

Friends unlatch the windows of our souls. They grip the drapes we've drawn around ourselves and yank them back to let God's gleaming light stream in. They pull and tug until the windows pop open and fresh, new breezes fill our musty hearts.

When storms throw trees across our path, a friend will lend her strength to haul the logs away. Friends are not fazed by our roadblocks. They come equipped with chain saws. They help us chop our obstacles like firewood then strike a match to them. They make sparks fly up from the flames. They say, "Why

a *love* that surpasses all human knowledge.

My forever love, *Jesus*

—Ephesians 3:17–19

Friends possess remarkable keys. They open the locked doors of our lives. They give us entrance to places we'd never dare go by ourselves. They fling wide the gates of lush, secret gardens. They take us to treasure rooms glistening with gifts we're sure we don't deserve.

Friends unlatch the windows of our souls. They grip the drapes we've drawn around ourselves and yank them back to let God's gleaming light stream in. They pull and tug until the windows pop open and fresh, new breezes fill our musty hearts.

When storms throw trees across our path, a friend will lend her strength to haul the logs away. Friends are not fazed by our roadblocks. They come equipped with chain saws. They help us chop our obstacles like firewood then strike a match to them. They make sparks fly up from the flames. They say, "Why

not sit awhile and warm yourself by this nice fire?" When the smoke clears, friends pass out coat hangers and feast with us on roasted marshmallows until the last ember dies.

Friends have sight where we are blind. They are guides through the jungles of our past. They are fearless to face the dangers we know lurk beneath the brush. Friends hack and slash at the wild, clinging thoughts that bind us. With grace, they loose us from our blindfolds then tie them on branches, marking a trail for the future.

Friends create breakthroughs. The best ones are agents of God. Like him, they stand us in front of a mirror and introduce us to ourselves.

A genuine friendship is a heavenly present. It blesses our hearts because God's love is in it.

—Evelyn McCurdy

More than anything else,
Nancy yearned to be *loved*.

A Hug
for Nancy

"Welcome to The Logan," Joyce chirped as she raised her head from her paperwork to greet her new guests. "We're glad you've chosen to spend some time with us."

Joyce and Larry Coffin owned and operated a quaint home-style hotel near the boardwalk in Ocean City, New Jersey. At first glance, the two young women standing on the other side of the check-in counter seemed fairly typical of their summer vacationers. Both were in their early twenties, and they had come to The Logan for some relaxation and sun.

But as Joyce gave them their room keys and the standard instructions, she noticed that one of the young women, Nancy, kept her head down and eyes to the floor, obviously avoiding eye contact. She didn't speak a word but left all the talking to her companion. Uncomfortable with Nancy's glaring silence, Joyce was relieved when the two women departed for their room.

The next morning when Nancy came through the reception area, Joyce smiled warmly as she offered a morning greeting. "Hi, Nancy! How are you this morning?"

Nancy returned her greeting with stark silence.

Maybe Nancy hadn't heard her. She tried again, "Did you sleep well?"

Still no response.

Undaunted, Joyce made another effort, "You must have slept well because you look so bright-eyed and bushy-tailed!"

Joyce's cheerful words were met with more awkward silence. Not knowing what else to say, Joyce was relieved when Nancy's friend appeared and rescued Joyce from her fumbling monologue. The two women headed for a day on the beach, and Joyce returned to her duties.

Over the next few days, Joyce made a deliberate effort to converse with Nancy. Although Nancy never spoke a word, a weak smile or uneasy giggle would occasionally escape her lips. It seemed as if she wanted to let Joyce in but didn't dare.

steadfast friend

A Hug for Nancy

Something about Nancy pulled at Joyce's heart. Why had Nancy built such a barrier between herself and the rest of the world? What had caused her to retreat into silence?

Soon it was time for the two unlikely friends to check out and return to their homes in Pennsylvania. As they walked out of the hotel, Joyce felt an urgent need to do something to break through Nancy's self-imposed shell. Running up to her room, Joyce frantically searched for some token she could give Nancy. As she looked around her room, she silently prayed, *Lord, is there something I can give Nancy to let her know you love her?*

Finding a small gift, Joyce hurriedly wrapped it and ran outside, hoping it wasn't too late. She breathed a sigh of relief when she spotted the two women loading their things into Nancy's 1978 Buick Skylark.

"Wait, Nancy! I have something for you. I just wanted you to know that you are special and that God loves you. I'm glad you came." As Joyce handed Nancy the trinket, she felt compelled to accompany it with a big hug. As she wrapped her arms around her shy, perplexing guest, Joyce felt as if she were hugging a lifeless mannequin.

Nancy was obviously taken off guard by the hug but maintained her unresponsive exterior as she abruptly and silently retreated into her car. As the car left the loading area, Joyce prayed, *Lord, I feel so helpless and frustrated. I tried to show her your love, but I failed. I so wanted to hug her hurt away, but I was naive to think I could make a difference with such an insignificant gesture. You know what makes Nancy hurt and what will heal her. I'll never see her again, but you can be with her always. Please wrap your arms of love around her and keep her in your care.*

Several times during the months that followed, Joyce felt prompted to lift Nancy's unknown hurts to her all-knowing heavenly Father. Her prayers were often accompanied by a longing to decipher the riddle of Nancy's silence.

Meanwhile, back in Pennsylvania, the effects of that one "insignificant" hug were beginning to bear fruit. Joyce's persistent kindness and simple hug sparked a major turning point in Nancy's life. A peek back into Nancy's childhood reveals why Nancy had shrouded herself in silence.

Nancy had grown up in what she considered a fairly typical Pennsylvania Dutch home. But Nancy's home lacked even the most basic displays of affection, and her parents strictly limited her social interaction. One of five children, Nancy never had a birthday cake or party. She wasn't allowed to participate in extra-curricular activities or go to

steadfast friend

slumber parties or have friends over to her house, and she couldn't date until after high school graduation. Nancy's parents took her and her siblings to church when she was young, but they eventually stopped going; Nancy and her sister occasionally went on their own. Nancy did have a few pleasant childhood memories of family vacations and exchanging gifts on Christmas morning, and she knew her parents hadn't neglected her emotional well-being intentionally; but the lack of affectionate expression from her mom and dad had deeply wounded her heart.

Her dreams of friendship had been dashed on several occasions when she'd dared to open her heart—only to find rejection. Lately, she had managed to maintain a couple of shallow friendships, but those activity-driven relationships left her hungry for more. She longed for someone who dared look beneath the surface. She wanted more than a companion for movies or shopping. She wanted someone she could trust with her pain.

More than anything else, Nancy yearned to be *loved*.

By the time Nancy checked in to The Logan, she was emotionally crippled. Fearing further rejection, Nancy had padlocked her heart and withdrawn into the safety of an almost silent existence. She spoke only when necessary to the few people she allowed inside her lonely, walled fortress. When Joyce had tried to penetrate her refuge with kindness, Nancy hadn't known how to respond.

But as Nancy thought back to Joyce's kindness and her surprising hug two months earlier, something warm began to stir in her heart. Not allowing herself to debate, she opened her desk drawer, took out a paper and pen, and began to write.

> Dear Joyce,
>
> You may not remember me. I'm the lady who didn't talk. I loved my time at your hotel this summer. You had no way of knowing it, but you gave me a very special "gift." Your hug was the first I ever remember receiving in my whole life.
>
> I know that God loves me and that I need to get close to him again. Thanks for letting him love me through you.
>
> I will never forget.
>
> > Love,
> > Nancy

As soon as Nancy put down her pen, the inner debate began. She was so afraid of appearing a fool and of being rejected once again. But something deep inside insisted that

steadfast friend

Joyce would make a trustworthy friend. As Nancy sealed and mailed the letter, she hoped against hope that Joyce hadn't given up on her and would write back.

Several days later, as Joyce shuffled through a large stack of mail, she came across a letter that had been forwarded from The Logan to their winter home in Maryland. She puzzled over the unfamiliar name and address as she slit the envelope open.

As Joyce read Nancy's brief letter, tears streamed down her cheeks. Her receptive heart was quick to pick up on the tentative plea for friendship written clearly between the lines. Joyce responded immediately, and a special, long-term friendship was born.

Future trips to Ocean City were always spent with Joyce at The Logan, and over time, the warm, caring woman trapped inside Nancy was set free. Reminded of God's love through the embrace of Joyce's arms, Nancy slowly learned to trust again. Through the years Nancy and Joyce have continued to exchange letters written on "hugs" stationery. Several times a year they talk on the phone. They frequently exchange little "hugs" gifts, and they faithfully remember each other in their prayers.

Today, almost twenty-five years after that first hug,

Nancy is a totally transformed person. It's as if someone gave her a heart transplant. She enjoys chatting on the phone, is active in ministry, and looks forward to graduating from Bible school. Nancy is now so outgoing that she even talks, shares, and prays with perfect strangers. And when she visits her seventy-three-year-old mother, she expresses her love with an extra big hug.

"Never in a million years would I have suspected that God would use such a small effort on my part to bring about such big results," Joyce reflects. Joyce has no doubt that it was actually God who hugged Nancy that summer day in front of The Logan. He simply borrowed her arms.

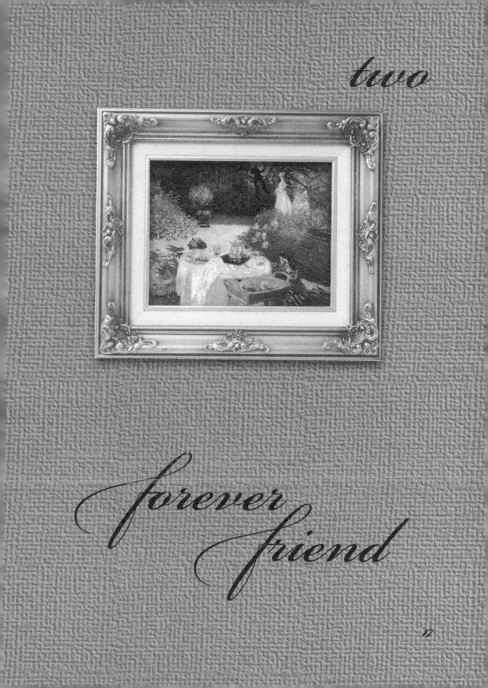

forever
friend

*L*ove as I have unconditionally loved you.

I demonstrated the very essence of **true** friendship when I *willingly* laid down my life for you.

What blessings I have waiting for you. *Think about it—*

I'm living *within you!* I've **reconciled** you to my Father!

Now, you can enjoy a wonderfully exciting friendship with the Most High God through me —forever!

Love,
Your  *Messiah and Friend*

—John 15:12–13 TLB;
Romans 8:11; Romans 5:10–11

We've heard how the heat of battle can take mere soldiers and turn them into soul mates. Somehow, the fire of affliction fuses a bond between those who might, under "normal conditions," overlook or even avoid each other.

It seems the strongest and most enduring friendships are not necessarily the oldest ones. They're often those forged in the furnace of adversity. Maybe this happens because emergencies heighten our senses and, at the same time, make us vulnerable. Tough challenges reduce our reserve. They disarm our defenses. They ripen our hearts for relationship and lay our souls open to intimacy.

Sometimes, we're so wounded that we'll take help from anyone. Like a drowning victim, we thrash and choke and beg for air. Then, out of nowhere, comes a hand. At that moment, we don't care whose hand it is or where

it's been. It's all we've got, so we grab it.
And once we're on land and breathing again,
we shake that hand until our arm falls off. That
hand was our hope. And a relationship blooms
from a rescue.

Crisis breeds camaraderie. It turns total strangers
into cherished confidants. We're relieved to dis-
cover someone whose experience bears a striking
resemblance to our own. It gladdens us to know
we're not alone. We will always enjoy our childhood friends—the ones we lived next door to or
met on the playground in second grade. But
when we grow up, our needs change and
God provides friends of a different kind—
friends who are formed in the School of
Hard Knocks, companions who've
come from the classroom of life.

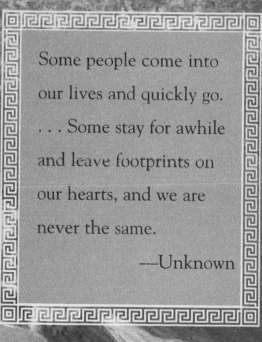

Some people come into
our lives and quickly go.
. . . Some stay for awhile
and leave footprints on
our hearts, and we are
never the same.

—Unknown

Helen discovered the secret
that we are only able to love
others because God first loved us.

Unlikely Friends

The first meeting of Mrs. Helen Correa and Mrs. Lillian Allen was anything but friendly. Their husbands, Mac Correa and Joe Allen, both worked at WYCO Tool Company in the Chicago area. The two wives met for the first time at the annual company holiday dinner in 1949. As Mac Correa scanned the festive room full of fellow employees and their spouses, he was surprised to spot the Allens. "Hey, honey, look; that's Joe and his wife—the couple I told you about," Mac whispered as he pointed across the room to identify the Allens. "Remember, they're the couple whose six-year-old diabetic daughter just died." He briefly recounted the tragic story of how a medical intern, in a rush to leave for a Christmas party, had accidentally administered a fatal overdose of insulin to the Allens' little girl.

On the other side of the room, Mrs. Allen felt like a fish out of water in the jolly holiday atmosphere. *Why did God take our precious Carrie?* she silently asked for the thousandth time as she tried to maintain her composure. *How can all these people be so happy when my world has just fallen apart?* She tried to pretend she was listening to the meaningless babble that surrounded her. Everyone was talking about their families and the festive gatherings they'd had on Christmas day. Each mention sent a stabbing pain through her already shattered heart. And then there were the empty efforts at condolences. She knew they meant well, but none of these people knew her or her pain. No one knew what to say, yet everyone felt they needed to say something. The resulting comments were stilted and awkward—anything but comforting. She hadn't wanted to come tonight, but several friends had insisted that it would be good for her to get out since she had been cooped up in the house with her other four children since Carrie's burial the previous week.

Mrs. Correa observed Mrs. Allen from a distance. *What is she doing out in public so soon? Her poor little daughter was just buried on December 23rd. How inappropriate for her to be here for a holiday celebration.* As she scrutinized Mrs. Allen's

forever friend

behavior from across the room, the sympathy and compassion Helen had felt when she first heard of their tragedy drained from her heart. She was absolutely appalled when she caught Mrs. Allen cracking a half-smile a few times throughout the evening. *How could a loving mother smile so soon after losing a child?* Mrs. Correa was unquestionably confident that she would never smile again if she lost her child. *And she is supposed to be such a religious woman. Mac said she was downright fanatical! What kind of religion would let a mother be out partying at a time like this?*

Meanwhile, Mrs. Allen's first impressions of Mrs. Correa were reciprocally negative. In her eyes, Mrs. Correa was nothing but a "harsh-looking, overpowering, heavily painted, cigarette-smoking, worldly feminist."

When they were formally introduced later that evening, the interaction was extremely awkward. Trapped by civilities, neither of them could hide their disdain. Both were relieved at the conclusion of their brief encounter. Quite obviously, they had absolutely nothing in common. Even more convinced that the Allens were "religious extremists," the Correas made it a point not to have anything to do with them outside the necessary contact between the husbands on the job.

But in April of 1953, the Correas' world crumbled. Their four-year-old son and only child, Jerry, lost his life to an incurable kidney disease.

When Joe Allen told his wife of the tragedy and suggested they go to the wake in West Chicago, Mrs. Allen felt as if she'd been hit by a truck. The news stirred up painful emotions, and the thought of seeing another young child in a tiny-sized coffin was almost more than she could bear. But, like her husband, Mrs. Allen knew in her heart that it was the right thing to do.

When Mrs. Correa saw the Allens, she flashed back to their only meeting over three years ago at the Christmas dinner. Mrs. Correa now recounted Mrs. Allen's smile in a different light. Overcome with grief she hopelessly cried out, "Mrs. Allen, how did you ever live through the experience of losing your daughter?"

Mrs. Allen softly replied, "It was only with God's help that I was able to survive."

About a week after Jerry's burial, Mrs. Correa was surprised to receive a letter from Mrs. Allen inviting her to lunch. Even though she was desperately hurting and in need of comfort, she wanted nothing to do with this religious fanatic and the glib panaceas she might offer. As she con-

forever friend

sidered how to turn down the invitation politely, another piece of paper tucked inside the envelope caught her eye. She hesitantly unfolded the beautiful stationery and began to read . . .

> He is a little flower
>> plucked from this world of woe.
> He will blossom in God's garden,
>> and by his love will grow.
> Left from the evil of this world,
>> his life shall perfect be,
> Dwelling in the mansions all through eternity.
>
> Oft times our hearts are troubled,
>> and oft we wonder why
> Our little ones from heaven
>> must leave our homes and die.
> And yet we cannot think of them as dead—
>> but just away,
> For they are with our blessed Lord
>> forever more to stay.
>
> So when your heart is heavy
>> and sorrows bend you low,

In the secret of His presence,
    you'll find the heavenly glow.
He will give new strength for every day
    and all our sorrows share.
So weep not loved ones for him;
    he's in our Savior's care.

The beautiful poem had obviously been written by Mrs. Allen after Carrie's death. It had been modified for Mrs. Correa's son, Jerry. Tears welled up in her eyes as she read the tender words of hope, and when she had finished reading, a little door in her heart opened—just a bit. *Anyone who could write a poem like this after her child died must have something special.* Grief-stricken, lonely, hopeless, and without direction, she decided to accept Mrs. Allen's invitation and find out if she had any help to offer her. *My life is meaningless; if Mrs. Allen turns up empty, I will be no worse off than I already am.* When Jerry died, Mrs. Correa's whole world had died with him; this was the first glimmer of hope she had felt.

When Mrs. Correa arrived for lunch, she saw that the table had been painstakingly set, as if it were being featured in *Good Housekeeping Magazine.* Mrs. Allen's care showed in every detail—from her dress, to her hair, to the fine china,

forever friend

to the flowers in the vase, to the colorful presentation of the table and the scrumptious food. The extra effort caught Mrs. Correa off guard.

But Mrs. Correa was pulled back to reality when her hostess sweetly asked, "Would you mind if we thanked God for the food?"

Of course she minded. *There she goes again with her religious mumbo-jumbo*, she thought as she quickly located the two exits out of the house. *Still*, she reasoned, *it is a lovely meal, and I don't want to appear ungrateful.* So she kept her annoyance to herself and bowed her head.

They hadn't even gotten to dessert when Mrs. Allen purposefully reached behind the server and picked up a Bible. "Would you mind if we read the Bible together?" Without waiting for a response, she opened the book and began reading passages about heaven. Mrs. Correa's anxiety was growing by the minute. *This is going too far. This religious woman is out of control!* But as Mrs. Allen read from the Bible in her lap, her voice was so full of hope and assurance, that Mrs. Correa was enthralled.

> For we know that if the earthly house of our tabernacle be dissolved, we have a building from God, a

house not made with hands, eternal in the heavens. (2 Cor. 5:1 ASV)

For our citizenship is in heaven; whence also we wait for a Savior, the Lord Jesus Christ. (Phil. 3:20 ASV)

But according to his promise, we look for new heavens and a new earth, wherein dwelleth righteousness. (2 Pet. 3:13 ASV)

Mrs. Correa had never thought much about heaven before. But she knew the Bible was a special book, and if it said there was such a place, she now realized that Jerry must be there. Relief flooded her heart as she imagined her precious Jerry safe in the arms of Jesus.

Mrs. Allen stopped reading and caringly looked up, establishing clear eye contact with Mrs. Correa as she said, "One day Jesus is coming back to take all of those who believe in him to be with him forever." She lovingly but boldly confronted, "Will he take you?"

Caught off guard, Mrs. Correa defensively sputtered, "Well, I've attended Sunday school since I was three . . . I've taught Sunday school for years . . . I even sing in the church

forever friend

choir!" But as she added to the list, she could tell Mrs. Allen didn't seem at all impressed with her deeds.

Mrs. Allen continued reading, now from John 5:24, "Verily, verily, I say to you, He that heareth my word, and believeth him that sent me, hath eternal life, and cometh not into judgment, but hath passed out of death into life." As Mrs. Correa listened to this verse, she realized for the first time that Jesus was the only acceptable substitute for her sin. Nothing else mattered.

That afternoon of April 21, 1953, Mrs. Correa received the most important hug of her life when she invited Jesus to become her savior and best friend. This new friendship with Jesus would now eternally transform all other relationships, as it is the very basis of love.

Mrs. Allen now became Lillian and a dear friend to Helen Correa. Helen discovered the secret that we are only able to love others because God first loved us. He calls for us to examine all of our relationships through his eyes of unconditional love.

Today, almost fifty years later, my grandmother, Lillian Allen, and Helen Correa share a lasting friendship. Although separated by more than three thousand miles, they've discovered that "a lifetime is not too long to live as friends." Through the years, Helen Correa has enthusiastically shared her testimony at Christian Women's Clubs, groups, and with everyone she meets. As a result of the hug of salvation that my grandma shared with her, Helen's husband, Mac; their entire family; and many others have come to know Jesus Christ as their best friend too.

"I thank God that your grandma saw my need and cared enough about my eternal destination to get involved in my life and lead me to an eternal friendship with Jesus Christ," Helen gratefully shared with me. "Because of him, your grandma and I are forever friends!"

And thanks to their best friend, Jesus, they both look forward to continuing their friendship in heaven and to their upcoming reunion with Carrie, Jerry, Grandpa Joe Allen, my mom, and many other forever friends who have already gone ahead.

As Michael W. Smith sings, "Friends are friends forever if the Lord is the lord of them."

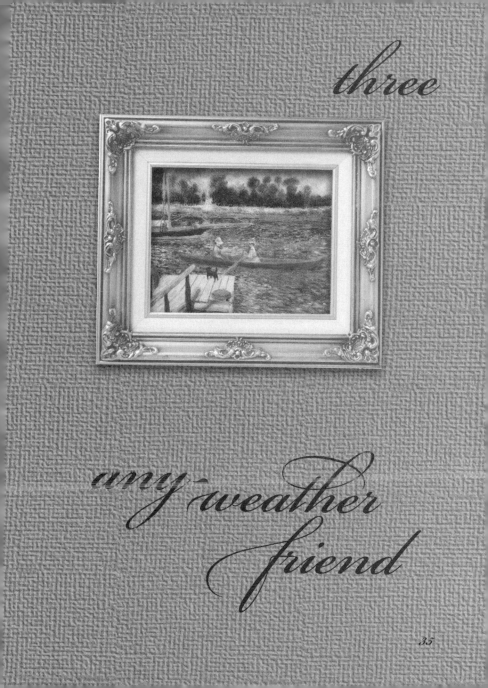

three

any-weather
friend

I've chosen you!
You are *holy* and *loved*.

May you consistently live your life with
a **heart** of compassion,
daily demonstrating *kindness*,
humility,
gentleness, and patience.

Choose to gracefully *forgive others* when
they **disappoint** you or **hurt** you—

just as my Son, Jesus, forgave you.

Most importantly, let love be the superglue that bonds all your relationships and friendships.

Love,

Your *God of Love and Forgiveness*

—Colossians 3:12–14

One of the best things about having a good friend is all the grace you get. You just sit around being you, and a good friend makes you think she wouldn't dream of having it any other way.

For instance, you can have a rotten attitude and end up saying things you're sorry for later, and a good friend will hardly be fazed by it. She'll act like it's no big deal. She'll just put her arm around you and say, "Don't worry about it. Everyone has a bad day now and then"—even if you've had ten bad days in a row.

And a good friend isn't surprised by your mistakes. She expects them. Somewhere, fairly early in the relationship, a good friend will find out the truth about you. She'll witness your weaknesses firsthand. And it's at this point that your friend, if she's really a good friend, will decide to stick by you anyway. Oh, in the early days she may have whined and complained a bit about your less than desirable traits, but before long, something grows in her and outweighs them—it's called *grace*. Then, instead of fussing about your ten-thousandth tardiness, she just plans for it. She brings a book or buys a paper or files her nails. And when you finally come racing up, out of breath, with a million and one excuses, she looks at you, smiles, and says, "Don't worry about it. Really. It's okay. I haven't been waiting that long."

The face of a friend reflects God's grace.

Real friends are those who, when you've made a fool of yourself, don't feel that you've done a permanent job.

—Erwin T. Randall

Despite all my shortcomings
and humdinger flub-ups,
my friends still loved me.

Forgiven Fiasco

"Come with us, Sue," I cajoled. Sue and I were close friends, prayer companions, and tennis partners. Sue's idea of camping is a comfortable room at the Hilton. You know—hot showers, soft beds, air conditioning, and swimming pools.

Sue *might* have felt okay about camping at a well-lit, just-off-the-freeway, security-patrolled campsite with flushable toilets and paved roads. But a canoe trip to a remote clearing in the forest was way beyond her comfort zone. No electricity or running water, the open forest for a rest room, snakes, mosquitoes—it was all too much. But after much cajoling and negotiating, Sue reluctantly agreed to go. "It will be a fun adventure you won't forget," I firmly reassured her.

The night before our Friday departure, I stayed up almost

all night packing. My motto in traveling is "Why leave the kitchen sink? It might come in handy." I like to anticipate problems and be prepared. But all my preparation was undercut when one of my friends (cheered on by my sister and another friend) decided at the last minute to become a self-appointed inspector and rifled through my backpack and bags, removing three-quarters of my "important stuff." My objections were to no avail, and we departed with a much lighter load.

In protest, I defiantly vowed not to speak on the drive to the forest. It didn't help my already challenged attitude that the three co-conspirators enthusiastically responded, "Do you promise?"

We finally arrived and quickly loaded the canoes. Just shortly before sunset, we pushed off from Katie's Landing. Sue, my cousin Jamey, and I were in the first canoe. I was designated navigator of our canoe since I was the only one in it who had made this trip before. My sister Pat, Terri, and Don (all of whom had been with me on our previous trip) were in the second canoe. Having a highly competitive nature and still a little incensed about having to leave my emergency supplies behind, I raced ahead of the other canoe.

any-weather friend

Less than an hour into our trip, we had lost all daylight. Our canoe was still in a substantial lead. Occasionally, we would pause and wait a few minutes in hopes that the other canoe would catch up. I wasn't thrilled about our breaks, but I agreed, since the breaks gave me the perfect opportunity to set off some of the smoke bombs I had hidden in my pocket. They created a magnificent visual effect—trails of colored smoke streaming down the river in the moonlight. Those snapping alligators didn't know what to think.

Despite our stops, the other canoe was nowhere in sight. But we continued on, confident that they would soon reappear. "How much farther is it? Are you sure you know where you are going?" Jamey asked.

"Don't worry, we can't miss it!" I assured them. "You see, the last time we canoed to this campsite at night we thought we would never find it. But then, we came to the well-lit ranger station. This nice ranger told us that our campsite was only a half-hour away on the left side." I continued, "So all we have to do is wait for the ranger station and paddle on for another half-hour . . . piece of cake!"

We continued our fast pace without a trace of the second canoe or the ranger station. After what seemed hours, my cousin excitedly reported that he saw the ranger station in the far distance. Later, he updated us, "Hey, I see a bridge coming up!" Knowing there were no bridges along our route, I was convinced he was seeing a mirage. I must admit that I was very puzzled when we passed under a bridge.

Later, Sue said she saw the light too. Finally, I saw the light. It was getting brighter and brighter. Soon the entire right side of the bank lit up. We were at a marina—not at all where we intended to be. We found a small restaurant, and having only four quarters between us, we seriously contemplated volunteering to wash dishes in exchange for a warm meal. Unfortunately, the kitchen had already shut down. We were surprised to learn that it was already past midnight.

By talking with some of the locals, we learned that we had drastically overshot our campsite by several miles. Assessing the situation, we further discovered that our canoe had all of the sleeping bags while our friends in the second canoe were carrying all of the food and tents. Worried that they would be cold without sleeping bags, we decided to backtrack and try to find them.

This time we had to paddle against a strong current. It was outright chilly for Florida residents. The temperature

any-weather friend

dropped almost 40 degrees that night. All of that stuff I was forced to leave behind would have come in real handy.

We came to a fork in the river and had to make a choice. Should we go right or should we go left? We went right—not sure at all that we had made the correct choice, but we had to keep moving or we'd never find our way. As we paddled along, the foliage became quite thick—like in one of those creepy, foggy scenes in movies shot in the Florida Everglades. Barely able to see a foot ahead, we were guided only by the dim light of our flashlight and the eerie glow of the moon shining through the trees.

Because I was sitting in the front of the canoe, my face was the first thing to collide with a massive spider web that bridged the width of the river. A few seconds later, I let out a death-defying shriek when a gargantuan spider crawled up my arm and neck and across my face. His legs were long and hairy and nearly spanned my entire face. Ugh!

"Look on the bright side . . . at least it wasn't a water moccasin," I tried to comfort my crew. Big mistake. From their horrified reactions, I realized that they hadn't been thinking about the possibility of uninvited poisonous snakes slithering from the overhanging branches into our craft. Until now.

To our dismay, the river path we had chosen got narrower and narrower and finally ended. We had to turn around and make our way back to the main river. Jamey and Sue finally decided enough was enough. Sensing a potential mutiny, I followed their demands and guided us to the side of the river. Securing our ship to a tree, we set up emergency camp.

Jamey conducted a snake and wild animal check. At first, we were thrilled to find my pup tent in the canoe. But, it didn't help because the stakes were in the other canoe. On the bright side, we were able to get a fire started with my two remaining smoke bombs, and we had *all* the sleeping bags. However, we would have gladly traded the sleeping bags for the tents and the food. We split a single beef jerky and a smuggled candy bar.

Exhausted from hours of canoeing against the current, the three of us just lay there motionless under the stars. Every so often someone would pipe up, "What was that?" or "Did you hear that?" in response to the multiplied sounds of the forest.

About an hour after we stopped, we heard a large rustling noise moving through the forest. Crackling leaves. Snapping twigs. Stammering, Sue asked, "A-a-re there

any weather friend

b-bears in these parts of F-Florida?" as we prepared to run for our lives.

Much to our surprise, Pat, Don, and Terri emerged from behind the trees guided by the smoke from our fire. "Where in the world have you guys been? We searched for you for hours last night. We had given you up for alligator bait!"

"LeAnn was playing with smoke bombs and must have missed the ranger station," my cousin tattled. Our three friends looked puzzled.

"It's a long story . . . I must have missed the ranger station while I was setting off the smoke bombs. We ended up at some marina and had to turn around," I sheepishly confessed.

"What ranger station?" Don asked.

"What do you mean 'what ranger station?'" I replied. "You were all on the last trip. Remember, after canoeing in the dark for what seemed like an eternity, we finally saw the light of the ranger station on the right," I recounted.

I concluded by their still puzzled looks that they had had some kind of a twilight-zone experience stripping them of their memory. I continued in an effort to jolt them back to reality. "Remember, the nice ranger was sipping coffee by his fire? He told us our campsite was about a half-hour down the river on our left. *Now* do you remember?" I frustratingly asked, still wondering how they could totally forget such an important detail.

Pat, Don, and Terri broke into hilarious laughter. "What in the world is so funny?" I impatiently inquired.

"You were looking for a ranger station?" Don questioned, laughing even louder.

"Now we know you're blind!" my sister added.

Much to my dismay, they insisted that there never was a ranger station or a ranger. My "ranger station," they said, was a tent pitched in the forest at the right side of the river. And my "ranger" was just an ordinary camper. (Unfortunately for me, he wasn't there this weekend.)

"They're just pulling my leg to get back for all of the practical jokes I've played on them," I said, still totally convinced I hadn't imagined my ranger. After we loaded up our sleeping bags and put out the fire, we headed for our designated camping site. It turns out, we were only about a half-hour short of our real camp site.

Shortly after we arrived, it started pouring. In fact, contrary to the predicted weather report of a sunny weekend, it poured all day. Everyone had nothing to do except rehearse the fiasco I had single-handedly created.

any-weather friend

Forgiven Fiasco

I was bombarded with complaints and subjected to hours of interrogation, like "How in the world could you have mistaken that tent for a ranger station?" Every detail of the scenario was examined and magnified under a microscope. Complaints of soreness from the ten extra hours of paddling and exhaustion from no sleep were laid at my feet.

I'd finally had enough of their harassment and laughter and slipped out of the tent unnoticed. Death by pneumonia would be better than this kind of razzing, I decided as I sat sulking in the rain. It took them about an hour to realize that I was missing.

Sue and my sister Pat snuck up behind me. "Hey, where have you been? Come back to the tent with us; you'll catch a cold out here," one of them said.

"It's all my fault! I'm sorry I ruined everyone's weekend. I'll just stay out here," I pitifully sniffled. Sue and Pat embraced my cold, rain-drenched body. "Hey, we're sorry for giving you such a hard time. It's okay. It was an honest mistake," said my sister.

"Yea, just think of the adventure we would have missed if you weren't along," Sue chimed. "Your friendship adds so much spice to my life," she said as she hugged me again. When we went back to the tent, they wrapped a nice warm blanket around me and handed me a cup of hot chocolate.

Unfortunately, however, Murphy's Law remained in effect for the rest of the weekend. I was in charge of washing the pots and pans, but it was dark and I was afraid of water moccasins down at the river, so I decided I would just put the lids on the pans and wash them in the morning. In the middle of the night, we heard loud, clamoring noises. We were under attack! It turned out to be a gang of hungry raccoons that took off with our pots and pans. Also, I somehow managed to lose a borrowed, two-hundred-dollar sleeping bag.

But I learned a valuable lesson about friendship that weekend. Despite all my shortcomings and humdinger flub-ups, my friends still loved me. But, the most important thing I learned was the truth of 1 Peter 4:8 that love and friendship truly cover a multitude of faults and differences. Isn't it freeing to know that we don't have to be perfect?

Today, when we tell the story of our adventurous camping trip we roar in laughter. And the story gets better and better each time we tell it.

P.S. After we finally returned to civilization, I contacted the other campers from the previous expedition who all verified that there was no ranger station. I was sentenced to a life of wearing glasses and contacts following a comprehensive eye exam. However, to this day, I still suspect a conspiracy. I'm tempted to retrace our journey in daylight in search of my ranger station, but we've never gone back.

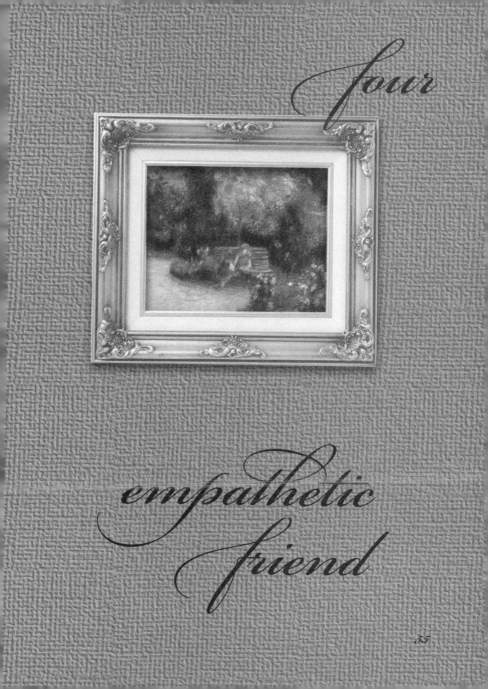

four

empathetic

friend

Prayer summons me!

Where two or more of you come together in
my name, I *am* there with you.

The prayers of a righteous woman
are **powerful** and *effective*.

Seek me eagerly and you *will* find me!

Love,

Your *Heavenly Father*

—Matthew 18:20;
James 5:16; 2 Chronicles 15:15

Right away, from the very first week, God seemed to know that the world would be too wild and wooly for us to make it on our own.

He looked at Adam's single self and announced: "It's not good for man to be alone." Then he went to work and fashioned a friend for him named Eve.

When Noah came along and the rain became a flood, God knew Noah would be going through some pretty rough waters. So, he sealed Noah up in the ark and brought his family along for the ride.

God gave Joshua to Moses as a companion for his journey through the wilderness. For forty years they walked and talked and checked their maps, until finally they found the Promised Land.

Daughter-in-law Ruth was God's gift to Naomi after the rest of her family had died.

In young David's most desperate hour, the Lord found Jonathan to be exactly the kind of friend David needed to make it to safety.

When everyone and everything was ripped from Job's hands, God allowed the comments of Job's comrades to keep him company.

And even as his only Son traveled dusty roads and sailed stormy seas, God flanked Jesus with faithful friends and followers.

The Father knew we couldn't make it on our own either. So he birthed us into families. But he doesn't stop there. Once we've been born again, he sets us up with a loving community that laughs with us and cries with us and prays us on to forever.

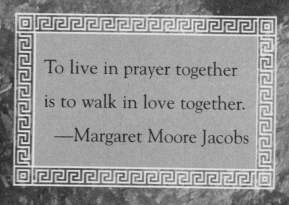

To live in prayer together

is to walk in love together.

—Margaret Moore Jacobs

The three friends clung to
each other and to the Lord
as their uncertainties escalated.

Shared
Pain

January 31, 1993, seemed an ordinary night in the small Kuna village of Pucuro, Panama. That quiet Sunday evening was hot and muggy, and Tania and Mark Rich were relaxing in their hammocks in their living room, each cuddling one of their small children.

Although she'd only been in Pucuro a short six months, Tania, a third generation missionary, felt right at home in the jungle. Nancy and Dave Mankins and Patti and Rick Tenenoff—their co-missionaries—had been invaluable in helping Tania and Mark learn the Kuna language and culture.

Tania finally got up from her cozy hammock to put the baby to bed. After eleven-month-old Jessica was in the crib, Tania realized it was beginning to get dark. Living in a village without running water or electricity, she decided to tackle the pile of dinner dishes and put the laundry away while there was still some light.

As she worked, something nagged at Tania, telling her she needed to put Tamra to bed too. But she had so much to do, and there was so little light left. Hurrying through her chores, the persistent feeling that she needed to get Tamra from Mark's hammock intensified.

Finally, Tania gave in and put the dish she was washing back in the sink. She walked into the living room, scooped her tired two-year-old into her arms, carried her to the bedroom she shared with her younger sister, and tucked her in bed for the night. Just as she kissed Tamra's cheek, she heard a loud commotion outside.

Tania's thirteen-year-old Kuna helper ran to the front door to see where the noise was coming from. But before she could open the door, three men in dark clothes and bandanna masks burst through the door, touting machine guns and yelling orders in Spanish. "Sit down on the floor! Put your hands up!"

Still in the room with her young daughters, Tania could only hear what was going on. Petrified, her heart stopped

empathetic friend

when she heard a gun shot followed by dead silence. Paralyzed with fear, frantic thoughts raced through her mind. *Have they killed Mark? Are they going to kill me and my children?* She wanted to run for help, but there was no escape—and even if there was, she couldn't leave her children. She began to earnestly pray in Spanish.

Tania heard footsteps throughout the house. The sound of water squishing in boots told her that these strangers have come from across the river. They were talking in Spanish rather than the Kuna dialect. "Señora, Señora," Tania could hear a man calling as he searched for her. She wanted to slip out of the bedroom so he wouldn't see the girls, but she was frozen with fear.

When the flashlight shined into the girls' room, Tania finally mustered the courage to say, "Here I am, what do you want?" They conversed in Spanish, and he instructed, "Give me your money . . . all of your money."

As Tania left the girls' bedroom with the man, she glanced across the kitchen into the living room and saw her husband lying face down on the floor with his hands tied behind his back. Mark started to struggle when he saw the man heading toward their bedroom with his wife.

Tania was relieved to know that her husband was still alive.

"It's okay, honey, they haven't touched me," Tania reassured him in English. At her words, Mark settled down.

Tania carefully followed all their orders. When they asked for sugar, she even volunteered a bag for them to carry it in. Then, as they instructed, she quickly packed a suitcase for Mark. Miraculously, Tamra and Jessica slept peacefully throughout the entire ordeal.

The sound of more gunfire rang out from across the village, and Tania knew that the Mankinses and the Tenenoffs had been invaded as well.

Just a few hours later, the three missionary wives sat huddled around Patti Tenenoff's kitchen table. Tania's two daughters and Patti's three children were asleep in a back room. According to village sources, all three husbands had been taken across the river on a trail leading to Columbia. The women and children were unharmed and together, but they were dazed and afraid.

The Kuna village where they were stationed was a small village of three hundred people in the middle of the rain forest. There was no police or military help. No telephones, no 911 emergency system. The captors had taken their only radio, which was their sole link to the outside world. Their

empathetic friend

mission plane wasn't scheduled to come for several more days, and they feared that the guerrillas might return to seize the plane if they waited. They were all alone—except for God and each other.

Acutely aware of their isolation from the rest of the world, they turned to God. "Lord, we need to know what to do. Please wake up people around the world and lead them to pray for us."

As the three frightened women prayed together, they felt a supernatural peace. Calmness and direction filled their hearts. They knew God was with them and that people were praying.

The only way out of the village was by canoe—and it definitely wasn't safe to maneuver the river by night. Nancy took charge: "I feel our husbands would want us to leave first thing in the morning." Tania and Patti agreed.

The three wives wearily bunked down for bed in the wee hours of the morning at Patti's house. After a fitful few hours of sleep, the women and children awoke early and prepared for the uncertain journey ahead.

Guarded by a Kuna man at each end of the canoe, the disoriented passengers left their homes with heavy spirits and headed down river to the next town. Tania, her two daughters and her Kuna helper, Patti and her three children, and Nancy sat in the crowded dug-out canoe, praying that God would intervene. Three hours later, they disembarked at another village. Here, they finally communicated with their sponsors, who promised to have an airplane waiting for them at the next village. The weary travelers reluctantly piled back into the canoe for another strenuous four-hour trip to meet the plane that New Tribes Mission was sending to rescue them.

When they finally reached their destination at 5:30 that evening, they were exhausted and spent, but relieved to find a Cessna plane waiting for them as promised. As the airplane took off and the three friends watched the jungle disappear below them, reality hit. They could no longer hold back the tears. They sat together, sobbing and holding each other, feeling guilty for "abandoning" their husbands and afraid for their lives. *Would they ever return to their homes and the Kuna friends they had grown to love?* The future loomed ominously.

In the following days they learned that New Tribes Mission had received a call from F.A.R.C., a guerrilla group in Columbia, claiming responsibility and demanding five million dollars in ransom for their husbands' release. The

empathetic friend

women knew that the mission couldn't pay the ransom without jeopardizing the lives of thousands of missionaries around the country. *How would the revolutionaries react when their demands weren't met? Were their husbands safe? Had they been fed?* The three friends clung to each other and to the Lord as their uncertainties escalated. All the while, the growing prayer support of people around the world surrounded and comforted them.

Leaving Panama without their children's fathers to return to the States was another tumultuous emotional cornerstone. But Tania, Nancy, and Patti held each other up and shared the strength of the Lord.

In the six long years since witnessing their husbands being forcefully dragged off into the jungle, Tania, Nancy, and Patti have experienced every gamut of feeling from faith, to frustration, to anger, to confusion, to despair, and then to hope again. They've been separated from their husbands for much of their married lives.

Mark Rich missed seeing his daughter Jessica's first steps and both of his daughters' first days of school. Imagine the sadness Tania felt when little Jessica innocently volunteered, "Mommy, I would give away all my toys, even Cubby [her favorite teddy bear], if it would bring Daddy back."

Both of Nancy Mankins's children, Sarah and Chad—who were living in the states at the time of the kidnapping—have married while their dad has been held hostage. Everyone prayed up to the day of each wedding that Dave would get back to give his blessing.

Patti's young son, Lee, offered to go live with the guerrillas so he could be with his daddy again. Nancy and Tania have supported Patti as she's asked the question David asked in the Psalms, "Why so long, Lord, why so long?"

During all the pain and heartache, the three women have grown to lean on each other as friends. Like no one else, they truly understand the gut-wrenching emotions each other faces on a daily basis. Each of them has experienced the peaks and valleys of faith as life continues without their husbands.

Together, they help each other through the painful birthdays, anniversaries, holidays, and everyday reminders of the men they love and dearly miss as their nightmare continues. The three friends have traveled around the world together, meeting with queens and presidents, petitioning for their husbands' releases. When Tania broke into tears, overwhelmed after another media interview, Nancy and Patti were by her side to encourage her.

empathetic friend

Shared Pain

Wherever Mark, Dave, and Rick are being held, their wives are comforted by the belief that their husbands are supporting and encouraging each other too.

Every morning Tania cries out to God, "Help me to go through this day joyfully, no matter what happens." During these long years of waiting together, the friendships of Tania, Nancy, Patti, and their children have been strengthened by the vast circle of friends around the world who lift them up to the Father every day in prayer. And they welcome new friends, like you, who will pray for their husbands' safety and return as well as for their children who desperately want their daddies to come home.

UPDATE: While there hasn't been any direct radio contact from the guerrillas since January of 1994, the Columbian guerrilla organization F.A.R.C. has claimed that Mark Rich, Dave Mankins, and Rick Tenenoff are still alive as recently as September of 1997. Tania, Nancy, and Patti request your prayers for wisdom and energy for the New Tribes Mission hostage crisis team, which has spent thousands of tireless hours trying to reunite their families.

Internet users can visit www.ntm.org for periodical updates and prayer suggestions.

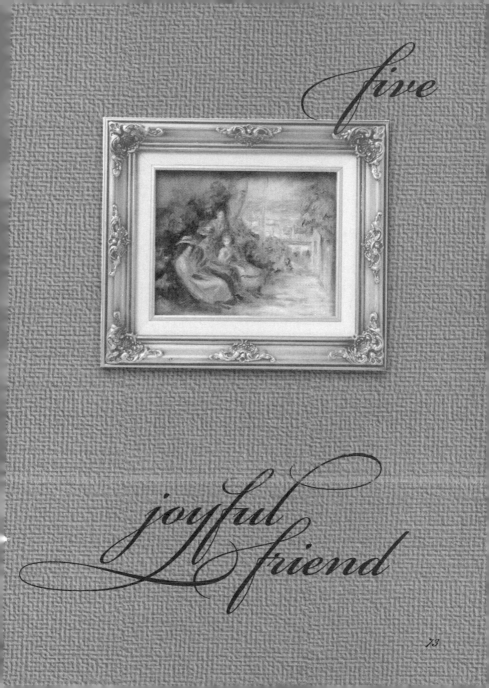

five

joyful friend

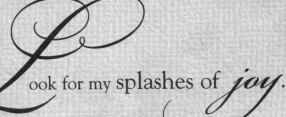

$\mathcal{L}$ook for my splashes of *joy*.

Laughter is good medicine—it's a great "shock absorber" for life's unexpected bumps. It helps take the monotony out of everyday life.

Don't miss out on the continual feast of a *cheerful* heart.

You'll see that a happy heart bubbles over into a smile.

And it's *contagious!*

Love,

Your *God of Joy*

—Proverbs 17:22; 15:13–15

F—a *friend* never *fails* to be *faithful*, even when others *falter*. She won't say, "You're *fat*," (even if you are) or *focus* on your *flaws*. She is the *first* to point out your *finest features*. A *friend* will *fortify* your *fragile frame*. She will *free* you to *flourish*. A *friend* will never *forsake* you.

R—a friend is a *rare* and *ready rock* you can *run* to in the *rain*. She will *rescue* you from *rushing rivers*—*regardless*. She will *revive* your heart, *refresh* your soul, and *reassure* you of *rapid recovery*.

I—a friend is not *impatient* or *impolite*. She will *inquire* about your day and *include* you in her plans. She will *identify* your most *incredible ideas* and *ingenious innovations*. A friend is *interesting*, *inspiring*, and *indispensable*. She is the keeper of your most *intimate* secrets.

E—a friend is a friend till the *end*. She is *eager* to listen and *easy* to talk with. She's your most *energetic encourager*. A friend will *embrace* you *even* in the midst of your most *embarrassing encounters*.

N—a friend will *not nag* (unless it is absolutely *necessary*). *Naturally*, she knows your deepest *needs* and is also *nice* enough to *nudge* you when you're *neglecting* your *nest*, being too *nosy*, or contemplating *nonsense*.

D—a friend is *devoted* and *dependable*. Her *destiny* is to *divert* you from *defeat*, and her *devices* for *depression* usually involve the *delicious*. It's a friend's *divine duty* to *drown* your *disappointments* and *dispose* of your *dismay*, and many times she *does* it in a most *delightful* way!

Laughter is the language of the young at heart. And you know what? You don't have to be happy to laugh. You become happy because you laugh.

—Barbara Johnson

A boring, seemingly wasted day was transformed into a treasured memory by the laughter of friends.

Garage Sale Escapades

Faced with an empty nest after her three grown boys had flown the coop, Pat sold her spacious 2,500-square-foot Laguna Miguel home and purchased a condo.

Preparing for the big move, Pat realized that over the past seventeen years, she had accumulated a house full of *stuff*. Since moving into her new condo meant losing 1,000 square feet, Pat had to choose between downsizing and wall-to-wall, floor-to-ceiling boxes. Pat opted for a garage sale.

After countless hours of sorting and tagging a lifetime of memories, the big day arrived. The garage was filled with a collection of bargains—appliances, books, records, knick-knacks of every imaginable variety, things her boys no longer wanted, and an assortment of odds and ends.

Huge signs were posted and a tantalizing ad sure to

attract bargain hunters had been placed in the local newspaper. With the help of her good friend, author and speaker Marilyn Meberg, Pat was armed and ready for the anticipated frenzy of garage-sale addicts. Everything had to go. Pat was eager to sell and prepared to make price-cutting deals to assure that her accumulated loot was hauled away. Pat and Marilyn eagerly took their stations and waited for the customers to pour in.

But Pat had forgotten to take one minor detail into account—the weather. California had been experiencing a heat wave, and this particular Saturday turned out to be the record-breaking day. The thermometer soared to a sweltering 103 degrees. If they had cracked eggs in the miscellaneous pots and pans they were trying to sell, the heat would have fried them.

Pat and Marilyn watched as one by one, cars began to approach the driveway, slow down, and pause. Occasionally, they could even see noses pressed against the air-conditioned windows as passengers carefully examined the wares, focusing and pointing at items of interest. But as the two women watched in dismay, each car drove off without actually stopping to ask prices or make a deal. Soon, the

joyful friend

"Warning—I brake for garage sales" bumper stickers would drive out of sight.

What a disaster! The sizzling heat was converting die-hard garage-sale junkies into drive-by shoppers. Pat and Marilyn sat in the sweltering heat of the garage, using garage-sale treasures as makeshift fans and guzzling frigid liquids in hopes of avoiding dehydration or sun stroke. Old LP records melted and warped in the sauna-like conditions, and colorful books faded under the intense glare of the sun.

In a valiant effort to divert their attention from the blistering heat, they rummaged through the discarded items looking for launch pads onto memory lane. "Remember when you gave in and bought this for the boys?" Marilyn asked as she picked up an old skateboard.

Pat grimaced as she held out an old pair of bell-bottom jeans. "Can you believe these are actually coming back in style?"

"Remember when we were on that health food fad and you bought this yogurt maker?" Marilyn chuckled.

By early afternoon, only one customer had braved the heat to examine their goods. Dripping with sweat and bored to tears, the two friends were still reminiscing over historic tokens when Pat spotted the old trombone case—a relic from her past. To Marilyn's amazement, Pat picked up the trombone and started blowing.

"Gosh, how long has it been since you played that thing?" Marilyn chaffed in response to the out-of-tune but recognizable song. "I didn't realize you'd ever had lessons."

Out of breath, Pat took a short break to explain that her musical career had started in the second grade. Because her seven-year-old arms had been too short to reach the trombone slide, she used to kick it with her foot. Marilyn laughed as Pat recalled how she had once missed the slide and accidently kicked the music stand off the stage and into the audience during a recital. "It's probably been a good twenty-five years since I've played."

"Hey! Can you play 'When the Saints Go Marching In'?" Marilyn asked. Rising to the challenge, Pat was determined to oblige her friend to the best of her rusty abilities. Although the gritty trombone slide hadn't been oiled in decades, Pat belted out the tune with enthusiasm. Suddenly, the dismal day was transformed into a slap-happy, giddy party as Marilyn began to march around the garage to the beat of the song, arms flailing dramatically as she conducted an imaginary band. Pat energetically joined the march, and

joyful friend

the two long-time friends pranced around the garage without a care as to what passersby might think.

Soon, the jocular ruckus began to attract attention. One of Pat's sons emerged from the icy air-conditioned house to see what all the commotion was about, but he quickly buried his face in his hands as he observed his mom and Marilyn laughing and cavorting around the garage with the old trombone. His chagrin only served to energize and encourage their slap-stick performance.

Carloads of people actually began to stop to see what all the excitement was about. Some even joined in the escapade with requests of their own. "What about 'Dixie Land'?" "Do you know how to play 'Daisy, Daisy'?" As Pat whole-heartedly tooted away, Marilyn, whose special laughter has earned her a reputation, laughed so raucously that tears were streaming down her face.

Everyone seemed rejuvenated by the jovial mood, in spite of the intense heat. One carload of passersby turned out to be a group of friends Pat hadn't seen in years, and they enjoyed a surprise reunion.

But despite the crowds their revelry drew, Pat and Marilyn barely made enough sales to cover the cost of the ad in the paper. One of the few items that did sell was her dad's set of old golf clubs, and she learned too late—just as she sold them for a "song"—that the set was a valuable antique. She ended up donating almost everything to charity, except the sentimental old trombone, which she decided she just couldn't part with. But the two weary women were still chuckling when the Salvation Army truck pulled away with a truckload of "priceless treasures." A boring, seemingly wasted day was transformed into a treasured memory by the laughter of friends.

Life is full of unplanned detours, less-than-desirable situations, and downright failures; but we can gain the upper hand if we'll latch on to a friend who can help us hurdle the obstacles of discouragement and defeat. So let your hair down a little and loosen up. Leap into the joyful journey God has tailor-made just for you. As my friend Barbara Johnson says, "The key is learning to look for the splashes of joy in the cesspools of life!"

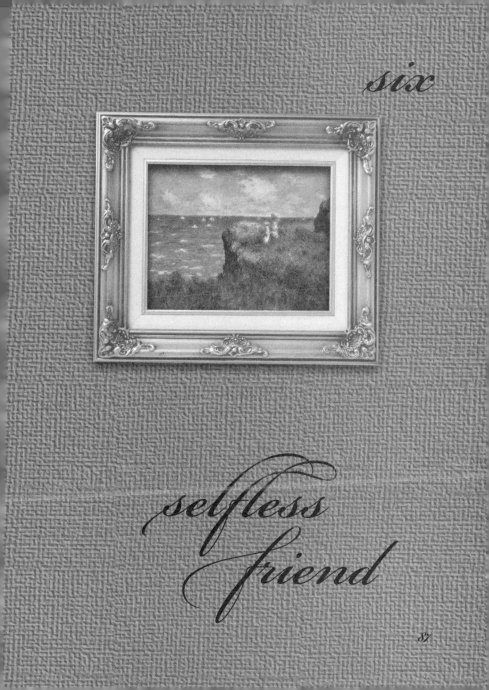

six

selfless
friend

I never intended for you to be a lone ranger.

You were *designed* for relationship.

A friend increases your yield, helping you reach the potential I've destined for you.

When you **fall**, your friend is right there to help you up.

Pity the person who doesn't have anyone to **stand** with her in hard times.

*S*ome said they'd pray. Some sent sweet notes. Others called to say they'd heard what happened and wanted me to know their thoughts were with me—which was nice and kind and thoughtful. But you were there. And I couldn't have made it without you.

Some folks brought food or watched the kids or offered a check to help pay the bills—and, of course, I was grateful for each gesture, each love expressed. But, you came through in a different way, at a deeper level.

Like no one else, you were there for me.

You let me rant and rave and ramble. Time after time, you sat with me and wiped my tears and washed my cheeks and whispered the words, "I know. I know. I know." And because of you, I held on.

Sometimes, you let me sit in silence and stare into space, because it seemed

But a three-cord strand with me at the center is not easily **broken**. Not even during earth-shaking, life-and-death trials.

Love, *Emmanuel, God with You*

—Ecclesiastes 4:9–10, 12

inspirational message

the right thing to do. Sometimes you encouraged me to talk. And you'd listen and nod, and your eyes would drip with fresh drops of empathy. You'd let me open up and dump out thoughts I didn't even know I had in me. But, there's one thing you never let me do—give up.

You said I could survive because you are surviving. And for what seems like the thousandth time, you'd hold my hand, look to heaven, and pray for me with the anguish of one who has been there too.

No. I couldn't have made it without you.

Friends are angels who lift
our feet when our own
wings have trouble
remembering how to fly.
　　　　　—Unknown

If there were such a thing
as a pain transfusion, her friend
would have willingly volunteered.

There for You

The fog that filled her head refused to clear. Somewhere in the distance, she heard strange, steady beeping and humming sounds—sounds she'd heard before but couldn't quite place. Trying desperately to concentrate, her mind began to drift, *Oh . . . I hurt. I hurt so bad.* She tried to move her arm, but it was too heavy. Now that she thought about it, her whole body felt as if it were encased in cement. She tried to speak, to call out for help, but no sound came.

Hearing voices, she looked up, straining to focus on five sets of eyes looking down at her. One by one, the nurses and doctors hovering above her said, "Hi, Sherry."

She tried to respond, wanting to call out for help, but no sound came. Alarmed by the throbbing pain in her throat, she panicked. *I can't breathe! I can't breathe!* Her breathing seemed abnormal, and then she realized she wasn't breathing on her own. *Wait! That humming noise is a respirator. Where am I? What's going on?* she silently screamed.

Something terrible had happened. Her memory, though vague, flashed back to sounds of sirens, people asking persistent questions, and the roaring sounds of a helicopter.

Confusion clouded Sherry's mind as she scanned the room for her husband Ken's loving face. *Where is he? What if something is wrong with him? Is he hurt?* Tormenting thoughts engulfed her mind. *Where's my precious Ken?*

Moments later, Ken's dad bent down and whispered words that confirmed her deepest fears, "Kenny's gone."

Sherry inwardly wailed, *No! No! He can't be! Jesus, I need Ken. He can't be gone. How can I live without him?* Soon, the pain medicine took over, and Sherry drifted back to sleep, praying that what she had heard was only a vanishing nightmare.

Later when she awoke, her mother was standing next to her bed, gently holding her IV-pierced hand. "Honey, I'm here for you," her mom assured.

Moments before her mom's arrival, Sherry had despondently thought of dying. But as she looked up at her

selfless friend

mother's beautiful smile and loving eyes, Sherry thought, *Jesus, my mother needs me. I can't die now. Please help me.*

Sherry used sign language to spell Ken's name to her mom and struggled to flutter her hand like a bird flying away, symbolizing Ken's death.

"I know, honey. I know," her mom responded sympathetically, patting her hand. Strengthened by her mom's presence, Sherry eventually drifted back to sleep.

Hours later, on the other side of the hospital-room door, Sherry Anne Frattini stood, trying to gather the courage to open the door and walk into the room. She'd come as soon as she'd gotten the news. She and her husband, Mike, had booked airplane tickets from Colorado to Cedar Rapids, Iowa, within hours of the phone call and had hurriedly arranged for someone to care for their children. She could hardly believe that her best friend, Sherry Jones, had been in such a traumatic accident.

The two Sherrys had met sixteen years ago during their junior year at Westminster High School. They were both trying out for the varsity cheerleading squad—Sherry Anne as a returning member of the squad and Sherry as a transfer student. Both girls made the team and instantly connected, becoming best friends almost overnight. Today, they still lived within thirty miles of each other, frequently interacting on a weekly basis.

And now, her best friend needed her like she had never needed her before.

Sherry and Ken had gone to Iowa for Ken's sister's New Year's Eve wedding. On their way to the airport for the return flight home, Ken's father cautiously slowed the van as he approached an ungated railroad crossing, but a line of dense trees obscured his vision.

By the time they saw the train emerging from behind the trees, it was too late. The train clipped and ripped off the entire right side of the van, sending it into a 360° turn before hurling the vehicle into a ditch.

Ken, his uncle, and Sherry were catapulted more than forty feet from the van into the twenty-below-zero weather. Ken's father and two other relatives suffered only minor cuts and bruises, but Ken and his uncle were pronounced dead at the scene. Unresponsive and barely alive, Sherry was airlifted to a nearby hospital and then quickly rerouted to the University of Iowa Hospital and Clinic, which was better equipped to handle severe trauma injuries.

Sherry's life-threatening injuries included a collapsed

lung, a bruised liver, extensive internal hemorrhaging, and a shattered hip that required eight hours of emergency reconstructive surgery.

Miraculously, she hadn't sustained any spinal cord injury or brain damage, but her body was shattered—she had broken a leg, an arm, three ribs, a clavicle, and her scapula. She also had multiple pelvic fractures and a dislocated shoulder. And to top it all off, Sherry had learned just two months ago that she had cancer.

When Sherry Anne finally stepped into the small, dreary hospital room, her breath caught in her throat when she saw her friend lying motionless on the stiff hospital bed. Surrounded by life-support equipment, oxygen tanks, and flashing monitors, much of Sherry's small frame was entombed in white casts and bandages. Blood oozed through some of the gauze. Metal pins protruded from her right leg, which was raised in traction. What skin was visible was swollen and black and blue. Sherry Anne audibly gasped when she saw the deep, jagged gash across Sherry's knee and leg, exposing the wounded flesh inside.

The octopus of tubes and contraptions extending from her friend's frail body only intensified her fears that she might lose her best friend. What would she do without her best friend? She needed her! Sherry's eyes were closed, but her intermittent moans revealed that her sleep was not peaceful.

Sherry Anne made her way to her friend's bedside. Tenderly grasping Sherry's hand in hers, she gently squeezed. Sherry opened pain-filled eyes. When she saw her dear friend, her eyes responded with a flicker of recognition. The tube in her throat prevented her from talking, so she feebly motioned for a piece of paper and pen instead. "Ken's dead," she wrote.

"I know, sweetheart. They told me. I'm so sorry. I know how much you loved him." The pain in her best friend's eyes cut through Sherry Anne's heart like a knife. At that moment, Sherry Anne felt she would do anything to make her friend whole again. Thoughts of her own needs fled. "I wish I could take your pain away and put it on me," she said. And she meant it.

And Sherry knew she meant it. If there were such a thing as a pain transfusion, her friend would have willingly volunteered. Knowing that she was loved so completely, so selflessly, sent a surge of courage and hope through Sherry's heart—and for a moment, her fear and depression lifted.

Over the next several days, Sherry Anne took up her

selfless friend

post beside Sherry's mother, who was a constant and faithful support for her daughter. Sherry Anne stayed faithfully by her friend's side, helping her process her thoughts, encouraging her to communicate on paper, and patiently waiting while Sherry painstakingly wrote her needs, feelings, and fears.

And when it came time for Ken's funeral, Sherry Anne stayed by her friend's side. Sherry had waited thirty-one long years to meet and marry Ken. So often she had shared with Sherry Anne that her marriage with Ken far exceeded all her dreams. She had been so content. And now, after only fifteen short months of marriage, he was gone, and Sherry was fighting for her life—denied even the opportunity to find closure with a final good-bye at her husband's funeral. Sherry Anne ached with her friend, feeling the pain of her shattered dreams and unfulfilled future family with Ken. She wished again she could bear some of her beloved friend's pain.

Eventually, it was time for Sherry Anne and her husband to go home. Their children needed them, and she had to get back to college. Although Sherry's condition was improving and the doctors now offered hope, Sherry Anne knew that her friend was not completely out of danger.

Leaving her best friend made her feel as if she were being torn in two.

After returning home, Sherry Anne called every day, getting updates and relaying messages through Sherry's mom.

And then the wonderful day came when Sherry Anne heard the sweet, familiar voice of her friend resonating through the telephone, and she knew in her heart that Sherry was going to make it.

One month after the accident, Sherry stabilized enough to be transferred to a Colorado hospital, only miles from Sherry Anne's home. Again, Sherry Anne was by her side.

One more month, and Sherry was released to go home.

Throughout the healing process, Sherry Anne was there for her friend. She cheered Sherry as she learned to walk on her own. She reminded her how to laugh again. She cried with her when the pain broke through her wall of composure. She helped her grieve and cherish the memories of Ken. She gently rehearsed with her the amazing power of God's grace. And together they celebrated the joy of learning that Sherry's cancer had gone into remission.

Today, Sherry still suffers physical pain from the accident, but she radiates God's faithfulness, sharing with oth-

selfless friend

ers the message that she was "broken, but not forsaken," and she frequently testifies to Solomon's wisdom that "two are better than one."

But as Sherry tells it, a precious moment that lit a flame of hope in her heart was the moment her friend loved her unconditionally and sacrificially and said, "I wish I could take your pain away and put it on me."

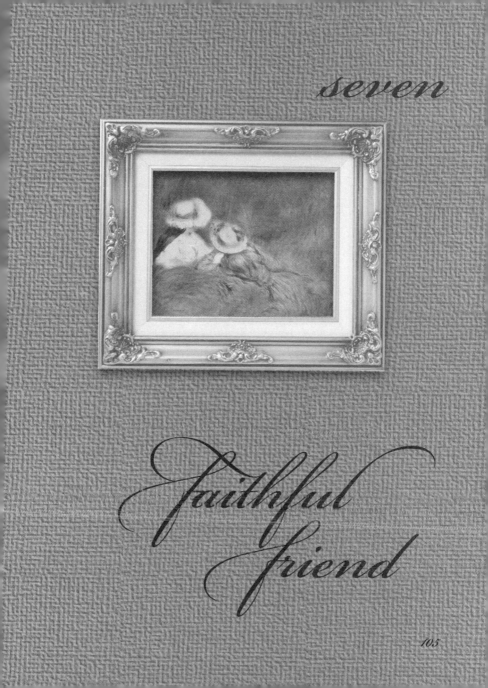

faithful
friend

*M*y Precious Child,

My all-seeing lamp searches out your very *spirit* and your **inmost** being. I know the real you that you sometimes try to hide.

I perceive your thoughts and even know what you are going to say before you say it.

If only you realized how *precious* you are to me! I'm **continuously** thinking good thoughts of you—

thoughts that outnumber all the grains of sand in the entire world.

Thinking fondly of you,

Your Creator

—Proverbs 20:27; Psalm 139

A true friend—

will listen for hours to your side of the story
and never once require the facts.

will tell everyone how great you are, even when
you've hurt her feelings.

never doubts you love her, even though you haven't
called her in eight months.

stocks her pantry with your favorite foods.

knows your middle name but will only use it when
she absolutely has to.

will tell you to freshen your lipstick then kindly
loan you hers.

will leave crazy messages on your answering
machine for no reason at all.

will not embarrass you in public.

will always come when your car breaks
down.

always has so much to tell you, even
though you've known each
other for thirty years.

will go shopping for herself
but come home with a
gift for you.

carries a good picture of you in her
wallet.

will always tell you to follow your heart instead
of your head.

remembers wonderful things you did as a child,
even though she wasn't there to see them.

would never encourage you to do something stupid.

is the only one who knows where you've hidden the
spare key to your house.

will feed your cat while you're gone even if she has
allergies.

is the name you always write on your application
next to "in case of emergency call_____."

would never talk behind your back even
though she'd have plenty to say.

will tell you things you really need to
hear, whether you feel like hearing them or not.

comes to you with precious messages like an ambassador
from God.

With the death of every
friend I love . . . part of me
has been buried . . . but
their contribution to my
being of happiness,
strength and understand-
ing remains to sustain me
in an altered world.

—Helen Keller

It was one of the hardest things
Sunnie had ever done, but it was
her way of honoring their friendship.

Last Request

Sunnie and Theresa were like oil and water. If cast for *Gilligan's Island*, Sunnie would play the bubbly Mary Ann —spontaneous and fun yet holding to conservative boundaries—and Theresa would play the gorgeous and flirtatious Ginger—always the center of attention and ready to push life to the limits.

When their brothers introduced them on Halloween night in 1984, Sunnie and Theresa became immediate friends. They even starred together in one of those comical music videos, singing what became their special song—"I Heard It through the Grapevine."

Eventually, Sunnie and Theresa moved into a plush uptown apartment, and these two fast-track, career-geared, materialistic yuppies became intertwined in a friendship that would ultimately alter their destinies.

Donned in their extravagant dresses, there was never a dull moment during their frequent nights on the town. Theresa was a magnet for men, flirtatiously leading them on. Sunnie would try to keep a straight face as Theresa gave alias names and bogus phone numbers. While living a fast, materialistic lifestyle, the hearts of both young women yearned for more.

Sunnie was always mothering Theresa, suggesting she change into a more modest dress or confiscating her keys if she thought her friend had had too much to drink. From the start of their friendship, Theresa teased Sunnie about being a "Holy Roller," but their friendship took a noticeable turn when Sunnie actually became a Christian at a Bible study two years after they met. Her conversion wasn't one of immediate, drastic changes, but it marked the beginning of a gradual makeover of her life and priorities.

While Theresa was respectful of Sunnie's beliefs, she was skeptical of religion as a whole, despite her strong Catholic family upbringing. She wasn't going to invest in something she couldn't see or touch, and she was turned off by hypocritical "Sunday" Christians. She was tolerant, but Christianity definitely wasn't for her. Sunnie was torn: She didn't want to offend Theresa or come across as preachy, yet she

faithful friend

longed for her best friend to find the same inner peace she was experiencing. Wanting Theresa to see a difference in her life, Sunnie adopted a low-key witnessing approach. She began doing little things, like setting all the stations in Theresa's car to Christian radio and giving her Christian books to read. But basically, they continued to accept each other "as is."

Neither of them expected Theresa's flirting to lead to a wedding. But in 1988, after Sunnie hoodwinked Theresa into serving as a Junior League Hostess for the delegates at the Republican National Convention in New Orleans, Theresa got the attention of Richard, a campaign operative for one of the presidential candidates.

When Richard accepted their offer to escort them to dinner, Sunnie felt like an intrusive "third wheel." As their threesome continued to spend time together over the next two nights, a slightly competitive rivalry began to develop between the two friends, and Richard became the focal point of their powder-room chats. From the love-sick look in Sunnie's eyes, Theresa accurately assessed that her best friend was falling in love. "Okay. I'll let you have him," Theresa conceded.

The next night, Theresa disappeared so Sunnie and Richard could go out alone. This continued for several nights, as Richard extended his stay. On the ninth night, he romantically got down on his knee and asked Sunnie to marry him.

The following April, Theresa, forever the faithful friend and good sport, was the maid of honor at Sunnie and Richard's wedding. She couldn't help, however, but teasingly conclude her reception toast with, "And Sunnie, don't ever forget I gave him to you!"

Marriage, distance, and eventually children didn't diminish Sunnie and Theresa's bond. They still talked almost daily, running up three-hundred-dollar phone bills, and frequently flew to visit each other. As Sunnie grew in her faith, her priorities continued to change. Although materialism was losing its grip on Sunnie, it still entangled Theresa.

Two years after their wedding, Richard's rededication to the Lord spurred on Sunnie's faith even more, and she became more bold in telling Theresa how God was changing her. In May of 1996, they met for dinner at a midway point between their distant homes. Shaken by the recent death of a friend, Theresa was in a somber, reflective mood. After a heavy discussion of death, Sunnie candidly blurted out, "Hey frogface, you have to promise that if I die you'll marry Richard and take care of my three kids."

Laughing at Sunnie's bizarre request, Theresa countered with a request of her own. "Well, my worst nightmare is that I'll look ugly in my coffin. I'd just die if they put me in some icky pale dress and my hair was a frazzled mess. You have to promise me that I'll go out in style!"

Getting serious again, Sunnie handed Theresa a book explaining what different churches believe. As they teasingly pushed the book back and forth between each other, Sunnie said, "Girlfriend, read this and pick a church." She was absolutely dumbfounded when Theresa nonchalantly responded, "Hey, how come in all of these years, you've never given me a Bible?"

After dinner, Sunnie immediately embarked on a search for a Bible bookstore. Together they picked out matching Bibles and Stephen Curtis Chapman tapes.

It was a night Sunnie would never forget. Sitting in Theresa's flashy black 1996 convertible Corvette parked in the driveway of Sunnie's sister's house, it finally happened: After years of praying for and witnessing to Theresa, Sunnie had the privilege of leading her best friend to the Lord.

They talked past midnight in the intimate, spiritual dimension Sunnie had always prayed for. "Come on, spend the night," Sunnie urged her friend. Theresa declined, saying she needed to go home, so they exchanged big hugs and tearful good-byes. They both understood that their close friendship had moved to a deeper level.

On Mother's Day, just two weeks later, Sunnie was out when Theresa's boyfriend called. When Sunnie came home, Richard greeted her at the door with the tragic news: Theresa had been killed in a car accident.

For a few moments, she disregarded the call as a cruel hoax. But as the tears started rolling down Richard's face, she realized that she had truly lost her soul mate. "Theresa was just starting her new life! How can this be?" she tearfully asked. Consoling each other in embrace, they cried, remembering the dear friend who had brought their lives together.

Later, Sunnie drove to Theresa's hometown and met Theresa's sister, Verlin, to help make the funeral arrangements. When Sunnie viewed the matronly light peach dress with a high lacy collar that had been delivered for Theresa's burial, she braced herself to execute her friend's unusual last request. "Please don't take offense, but Theresa would kill

faithful friend

me if she were buried in this." With Verlin's blessings, Sunnie got to work.

She spent over two hours restoring her best friend's curls, as Theresa's recent perm had been reduced to straw-like conditions by the embalming chemicals. She spruced up Theresa's lips with bright red lipstick and dressed her in her own favorite red-tailored suit, which Theresa had often borrowed, along with her pearl earrings and necklace. It was one of the hardest things Sunnie had ever done, but it was her way of honoring their friendship. When she completed the makeover, she almost sensed Theresa laughing from heaven. She even arranged to have their special "I Heard It through the Grapevine" video played at the wake.

During the eulogy, Sunnie had the opportunity to stand up and share about the life-changing decision that Theresa had made during her final weeks. Afterward, almost two dozen people approached Sunnie to thank her for sharing and to say that they wanted that kind of new life too.

At the graveside farewell, Sunnie experienced a roller coaster of emotions. While she rejoiced that Theresa was with Jesus, it was inconceivably hard to say good-bye to the person who knew everything about her yet still loved and accepted her. Daring to be vulnerable, they had shared things they had never told anyone else—and now those secrets were being buried with her trusted friend. But the blessings of their unmasked friendship and special memories, especially their last tender moments together, would be a sweet source of comfort to her lonely, lump-filled heart until their heavenly reunion.